THE LOVE STORY

A personal journey in the heart of Tibetan Buddhism

David Berger

This work presents a unique and contemporary approach, placing romantic love in the center of a spiritual transformation. It is nonetheless the fruit of long meditative practices in particular those of Tibetan Buddhism. One should consequently become familiar with its principles to better understand the ideas and the path presented here.

All rights reserved

CONTENTS

STRANDED	5
THE FAMILY	38
THE PATH	64
TRANSFORMATION	92
THE HAVEN	111

PART 1: STRANDED

The dark side on the moon
Is not seen by the eye
Only the heart
Knows of she

1

Rarely do we find romance applied to the spiritual path for it seems to oppose it by leading to a whirl of irresistible passions. In the past, even worldly conventions avoided it as a threat that led far from practical considerations. Nowadays romance has gained the upper hand, creating vast changes in sexual and social relationships. Yet it has not affected the way we see our inner world. Though sex has played a role in some spiritual quests, the idea of romantic bonds within us can appear ludicrous. Yet psychology has clearly shown that masculine and feminine elements reside within us. Whether it is Radha entranced by Krishna's flute, Orpheus braving hell for Eurydice or Psyche dying to see the face of her lover Eros, romance occurs in our earliest myths and stories we know as proof that it animated the psyche of the time. These myths indeed summon us to bring forth the realm of romance if we wish to know ourselves and grasp the dynamics that stir us. Understanding and integrating this wisdom brings forth an entrancing fulfillment for romantic love can blossom within us, the true form of romantic bliss which the aspirations throughout time shadow.

What an aspiration, this desire to unite in love! Pure delight is at our door, the eternal is unveiled, love reaches its apex in which we vanish with our beloved, we vanish from common day existence and the common vanishes also, whisked by a magic wand. Yes, all this is the echo of an inner truth humanity has yearned for from time untold, an inner state which is our due and seeks to blossom, seeks to transform our world and lead us from distress to the height of being.

2

In romantic love two beings who recognize each other feel the possibility of a boundless union fused by a love that weaves a reality well beyond the limits of this world, a love mysterious in origin yet a love that shines intuitively as a key element of existence. Romantic love penetrates our depths to unveil our dearest yearnings, shape our dreams and nourish our hopes. We know it by its presence in our lives which eventually permits us to apply this human passion as the greatest force of fusion and reconciliation to the shattered world it originated from, the realm of two beings of majestic proportion who lost their natural state of ecstatic union.

How can it be so unique, this love, to lead to such transformations? It unites the worldly to the divine. It dominates the worldly through the soothing of passions through the attainment of a long sought goal while shining in the divine through selflessness for the other, through losing oneself in love. It opens the portals of a dimension between worldly and divine of which it is the pivot.

3

As adults in a world constantly exacting more and more from us, transforming us and pulling us outward, it is difficult to know what is truly us and what has been created. We operate according to elements that are in constant flux and are ourselves ceaselessly changing. Yet we must find a suitable base for this continuity of being which we consider so evident. To find such a base we must go back to our first moments of life to see what was there that has lasted throughout, a thread that ran through the changes. Only such a thread could form the concrete foundation of our being, for clearly the rest came later. Of course, we do not remember. Studies, observations and theories lead to the general conclusion that we were but a bundle of experience. It is doubtful this bundle of experience knew it existed, felt, differed. Its only characteristic was the capacity to experience.

We could thus conclude that the newborn is but experience and in fact it is quite evident that experience does form continuity in time and could be taken as this foundation from which all-else results. It is impossible to detach anything from this base, even the most abstract and scientific thoughts. What permits us to define ourselves is our ability to experience and the ensuing continuity of experience in time.

4

It does appear that a dimension gives way to another and that this base of being, experience, gets lost in the complexity of the individual it permitted to create. While acknowledging the influence each stage of our life has on the next we usually see the newborn as having become the baby, the baby becoming a child, and so forth...But what if this was not so? What if these life stages remained buried within us, covered by new layers providing us the skills required to survive. In this case, since the basis of being, experience, forms the core of who we are, couldn't we then get back in touch with this nature buried by layers that had less and less to do with direct experience as they interpreted life in more and more complex ways? Though difficult to imagine, liberating direct experience is in great part what we will do here. Direct experience freed from its fetters can blossom once again, having never truly vanished, and can in fact exist side by side with all the various stages of life that occurred afterwards without contradiction, harmonizing them instead.

What is presented here is a path, a path leading to direct experience. The next few pages present the framework for the path, which is a way of seeing the world. If it appears far-fetched and hard to understand it should become clearer later when presented from the standpoint of experience, which is concrete and alive.

For the newborn, all is plain experience. Then arises an element apparently separate from experience which seems to be able to perceive experience from the outside, as if. Otherwise experience would not have been divided, the nature of the newborn would have remained ours and certainly no one would be conjecturing about it. Here we are however, and we are here only after the mind went ahead with perception, observation, and an effort to understand.

Perception was in some way always present. When we now speak of perception we generally mean this ability we have to grasp with our senses something that is separate from us, brought to us through the act of being able to perceive it. Yet at that basic level of the newborn perception was quite different, for there was no difference between perception and appearances. In fact, the world, the perception of the world, the experience of the world and being, they were all the same. There was truly no way to separate them. There was nothing between the world and perceiving it, nothing between this perception of the world and experience and nothing between this experience of the world and being.

6

Why then even bring up the notion of perception? Because it is part and parcel of experience and helps us understand it. Perception is present due to the continually changing nature of experience. Indeed, for change to occur, the present experience must dissolve even if for an infinitesimal fraction of time so as to reappear in a new form. We can compare this to a movie that appears to be projecting seamlessly but in fact consists of a series of images separated by tiny, unnoticeable intervals. Here however there is no film roll nor depository, it is perception that serves as memory. We can speak of a back and forth motion where experience is perceived and perception felt. At this primordial level no awareness nor presence. The energy of this exchange is most subtle and euphoric as well as being the foundation of what we are.

7

Unfortunately this alternation is not at all recognized as forming the continuity of experience. Rather the mind classifies the series of successive perceptions as forming one continuity and the actual experiences of them another continuity. Thus is born the appearance of two entities, one seemingly consisting of the object of experience and the other being the entity which experiences this object, oblivious to the fact that they are part of a unity where nothing ever remains as such, just like a coin flipping in the air. Rather, through the mind, an experiencing entity forming the series of experiences receives from a providing presence.

Throughout time, there's always been the need to give a name to that part of us which feels beyond every day life, resides in an unchanging truth and has often been considered the basis for sentience. The definitions vary but the word is often the same, and we shall use the same word here and name this receiving entity, "Soul". As for the other entity, the content, we could simply name it "World". Yet for the soul it is a presence that surrounds and penetrates from all sides so that the word "Lover" would be more appropriate.

We can see here how "Soul" and "Lover" have no absolute existence. They arise with the mind through its capacity to see similarities and classify them, a function of perception

8

Even though a kind of presence has been established, this new dimension is extremely pure for no self has yet surfaced. Our two entities relate in an extremely simple manner: the nature and the state of the other is known and a spontaneous reaction arises. It is thus a matter of reciprocity. In our complex daily lives we find it difficult to imagine a relationship devoid of words, reflections, hesitations.... yet it is where we should return if one speaks of pilgrimage, to this shore of simplicity where the world touches and affects she who knows him and gives him his very life and strength. The world, the lover, caresses the soul with a succession of waves that never cease to astonish, burying in the sand memories of past pleasures quickly covered by a new flood of joy.

This is a newborn, yes that very newborn who soils himself every two hours yet whose eyes are filled with limitless wonder, a wonder that naturally entrances and fills the hearts of all those around with love. What we see, truly, is the reflection of a sacred bond. Here ocean and shore meet. This shoreline is the love they share which now forms experience, the experience of a shining manifestation, the lover, drawing his splendor from the grateful pleasure he brings about.

9

In this analysis of experience, the choice of masculine and feminine is not arbitrary. Rather, classification by the mind gives rise to two elements which lead to the division of the world into masculine and feminine, elements to which we attribute various characteristics. Nor is the ensuing experience shaped by the lover to be known by the soul. We are not dealing here with a passive-active process, for the soul plays its vital part: Creation takes place only when it is received and reception determines texture. Thus the lover is only when the lover is received. This fully reciprocal relationship warrants saying that in fact giving is also receiving just as receiving is also giving, which may be the reason why the coin flips.

In everyday life a gift is a gift and remains so whether the outcome is a smile or a shrug. But here the gift is undefined until it is received. In constant flux, it goes from one to the other, changes in between as it disappears to renew itself in the form shaped by the shared process of giving and receiving. It is only when we lose sight of this process that objects appear stable and solid. In rare mystic moments a magical wand infuses them with a life and energy of their own.

This seemingly abstract truth is in fact not really absent in human relationships. A connection is never stable. The continuous and often silent exchange being two people shapes it. One feels the other, reacts to what is felt and in some ways shows outward signs of this reaction which the other then interprets, changing one's attitude slightly or at times radically. Nothing rigid and determined but rather a flux based on such things as our trust in the other, what we tend to perceive, what our expectations are and so forth.

10

Yet this intertwined bond of full presence and openness did not endure. The time has come indeed to face realities: True, the newborn often looks lost in wonder, yet when it cries, it is clearly suffering. This period of life is far from ideal, mostly when one takes into account all the efforts the parents put into soothing the child. Suffering appears in fact to be just as intense as joy.

When we look at a newborn and see a fragile and dependant body, we see the result of the limitations of the mind. By categorizing, the mind has created and continues to create entities that seem to exist in and of themselves, that take on the appearance of being stable and autonomous.

Let's look around us, if not at ourselves. We know everything around us is dependant and changing yet it seems to possess a stable and lasting quality. This principle of independence is epitomized by the body which grows with the feeling of being able to control its own destiny through its capacities, mental, physical and sensorial.

If the newborn finds in its cradle sorrow as well as joy, it is due to a journey the mind has led us on, for the appearance of false independence leads irremediably to the loss of well being, without us knowing it nor knowing how.

11

With the body then comes pain and a lack of faith in the process of life. This pain could have been felt at first as the waves of experience, a tempest, a momentary storm. But eventually the lover will react differently, in a more complex manner: He will try to prevent pain, an effort which will no longer have the spontaneity of the lover and another element will surface, the need to analyze and understand and with it the mental sphere. It will baffle the soul and lead far from the source of well-being.

It is here perhaps that we should draw a demarcation for here we leave our essential nature, we leave behind a truth devoid of doubt, questioning and planning. Before bidding farewell, let's once again grasp its essence: a complete lack of reflection which makes each moment of experience indivisible, coming from a single presence in a dimension devoid of self and solidity in which an act of love fulfills both parts of our being.

The subtle, penetrating and continuous exchange between these two components will be eclipsed and even before knowing how this beautiful shoreline will reappear only as dreams, myths, and underlying sadness. This is so for the lover will engage a pursuit to prevent pain, a pursuit which will end up being disastrous.

12

If we were fully immersed in a continuous exchange which was a source of natural fulfillment and maintained us in what we term the "present moment", what happened, why can we hardly remain more than a second in the dimension of experience before being carried away by a new wave of mental activity?

This new wave sets to resolve one or more of the various problematic situations at hand, thinks about them, tries to understand them, explores their every corner and consequence and so forth...We have certainly refined this process. Clearly a part of us, our rational mind, is attempting to increase pleasure and avoid pain in every day life. From where does it originate? Is it an element separate from the lover and the soul? To try to elucidate this question, let's compare the ties between lover and soul to those of an idealistic situation often reflected in some form or other in our imagination. A young girl, a young man and a perfect love where each is all the other desires. Then somehow the young girl falls ill. Love naturally takes on a dimension of care. The young man will do all he can to restore her back to health. But wasn't it always the case? Wasn't love in some way perfect care? Care here is but a facet of love.

In the same way, in this relationship within us that can be considered the rock bed of love, the lover will do all he can to heal the soul he sees in pain. This grand effort sparked our tendencies, mental capacities, ambitions and our emotions even. It has accomplished a lot, yes, yet as of now has failed in its original task.

13

Those who intuitively feel its limits and attempt to go beyond the sphere of comprehension hit a wall just as if one were to try seeing these letters without adding meaning to them. The mechanism of the mind once set in motion creates a reality that cannot just be dumped. Only by integrating it with the rest of being will it be transformed from prison to abode, thus allowing a return to the previous layers and a taste of the intensity of experience without having to lose contact with the creations of the mental sphere. In order to do so we must understand what understanding really is, that is we must turn understanding upon itself while until now it has been directed away from itself. It is for this reason that we returned to the moment when the process of analyzing was born, to become aware of what gave it birth, what unites it to the primary principle of being and redeems it, what permits us to strip it of its destructive and harmful elements and integrate it in our being, neutralizing the harm it has done.

Just like a man who, though accused of a crime, remains calm because he knows he was only trying to do good, all the harm the mental sphere may have caused can be cleansed in the baptism of the return to its source. It is love that gave it birth, natural love toward the soul and the desire to still her pains. It is indeed what turned attention away from her, to understand and with very honorable intentions change the course of things.

14

Unable to still her pains and feeling less and less able to fulfill while before his feather-like touch sufficed, the lover started doubting himself. From this doubt arose the need to find an answer. What was simply authenticity and spontaneity became an effort, and with this effort were born our mental capacities aiming at analyzing, understanding and resolving.

Many consider the mental sphere a savior, extirpating us from the fate of animals and bringing comforts beyond counting. It is however just fending for oneself, leaving behind an ugly trail. The toll includes grotesque and cruel ways of raising and slaughtering an unimaginable number of animals often under the pretext that they do not have a soul since they don't think. Its toll includes also the spreading devastation of a whole planet on the verge of an ecological disaster, and the possibility that the mental sphere will do here what it is doing in us, developing an intelligence which, though created by humanity, may end up controlling it. To this we can add that it provides no true well-being, cutting instead its source by separating us from our soul, home of authentic experience.

So let's look at things from the point of view of the soul. She sees a presence who was but tenderness and attention turn into some faraway presence locked onto itself, it seems. She would love for him to forget and come back as her pains are nothing compared to the sorrow that is taking hold of her. For indeed now solitude settles in, even if she is not yet truly alone but with the thick fog that her companion has become. But too late. The newborn is gone, the baby cries out, and the child begins exploring.

15

Let's illustrate the kind of situation that is occurring here with a pond fed by a source. If the water level dips a mechanism is triggered to add water and reestablish optimal level and then stops. This is a very common kind of mechanism, a feedback system. If we were to compare the water to the lover, the waterbed to the soul and the optimal level to a feeling of completeness, we see that we have fundamentally within us such a system, permitting the lover to vary his influence to fulfill his companion's need or in more objective terms for the world to fulfill experience. But what would happen if a hole were to start emptying the pond? The mechanism of course would have to work in a more continuous and regular manner. Here the hole can be paralleled to the doubt that plagues the lover and lessens his capacity to fulfill. Finally, an extreme situation would occur if the hole got bigger when the mechanism is working. The result would then be the opposite of the desired result. This is what happens once the mind tries to understand, for it draws the attention away from the soul towards oneself without realizing that what fulfilled her most was his constant attention and presence. These keep fading, leaving the soul in distress.

No need here of a devil nor of a god to create a hell. It only took a certain irony, a quirk in our nature to change love to tragedy.

16

When we speak of the lover locked unto himself and of the loneliness of the soul, it would be easy to deduce that this gradual separation led to the development of selves, each no longer seeing the other but oneself instead. It is not that simple. True, the lover's attention goes from the soul to itself, but this can only occur through the intermediary of the soul. The lover sees himself in her, he sees how she feels him. When he pays attention to his presence in her instead of to her, it creates the appearance of a self. It is no coincidence then that the words reflection and thought are interchangeable. In fact, the self can only exist and function through a reflection. It has no innate awareness. Unfortunately, all the intelligence at its disposal has not enabled it to grasp this, and now even if it could it wouldn't want to. Even at that instant when the self is born in an attempt to change things, it does not understand that it exists dependently as reflection only and that a clearer perception of the self depends upon a greater neglect of the soul, just like turning a glass surface into a mirror reflects yet hides things behind it. If we follow this analogy the soul eventually would turn into that thin silvery layer which gives the mirror its brilliancy. Thus the self, which arose to help the soul, buries her.

17

At first the self appears as but a stain in the lover, but with time it spreads to finally eclipse him. Being goes through a transitional period during which Soul and Lover attempt to maintain their world, to no avail as the rise of the mental sphere increases doubt followed by fear, the soul's reaction to seeing her lover's presence fade away.

She lives only through him so when his presence slips away the reaction is natural and immediate, fear, loss. This reaction will then increase the doubt the lover has about himself. Doubt is what led the lover to turn to himself and from this moment on to get lost in the labyrinth of the mind. The soul feels her lover who is all to her become first a stranger then an intruder and last persona non grata. The relentless rise of doubt and fear paralyses the lover and permits the self to gradually take control of the creative element and to become whether the soul wants it or not her new lover.

She has no choice, no real door she can close, no other place to go, she hides, in fact she herself contributes to the mirror by becoming invisible, turning thus into that thin silvery layer which hides her from the mental dimension, incomprehensible to her and the very world which snatched her lover away. Here ends the dynamic process in us which was the source of innate joy. It sinks into oblivion taking with it the two purest parts of us. Henceforth the self will get back from a stilled soul its own creation.

18

Emphasizing the self, then, leads away from joy and advice not to do so is far from arbitrary. The self is doubly bound to failure when it comes to fulfilling its purpose which is to bring constant joy. Its very presence opposes it, being the reason for the sorrow felt by the soul. Yet it does not realize it at all and tries by all means to bring about joy without understanding that the soul it sees is but a facsimile reflecting in the surface that hides her, for the mental sphere which is now dictating reality operates solely through conceptions. The soul no longer has any real exchange with this world. She rejects this presence which used to fulfill her. This rejected presence returning to its source without being enjoyed leads to the feeling of existence. When the source perceives it, it identifies with it and at that moment "I" and "me" are born, the origin being "I", the observer that triggered the mental dimension, and the reflection is "me", the observed, imbued with fear and doubt. The self here is composed of a rejected presence maintained in the reflective circle of "I" and "me". With time, "me" and all its characteristics becomes the self's dominant element.

This self has purpose and is constantly evaluating itself. It is passive yet attributes to itself all the processes and results of actions. Why? Because it is born of doubt and evaluation and thus it is in that dimension that it functions. Its judgment is the master, the verdict that sets all the other elements in motion. Just like a society functions according to certain laws that are fully passive yet regulate it, being functions according to the laws and verdict of the self, who also has no real basis for existence and yet controls everything. What gives it power is the presence now centered on it, originally the presence of the lover providing to the soul. In a way, we could say that the "me" took the place of the soul if we consider that the "I" provides to its own reflection, "me", in the same way that the lover provided the soul. When attention was centered on the soul, a reality existed, the original reality. When attention centered on "me", another reality was created, artificial reality.

20

The self, whose very presence opposes the task of bringing harmony back, finds itself in an untenable position which colors its world. The best way then to handle the situation is to forget, to turn away from whatever would recall this innate conflict. Forgetting only increases the distance between the basic reality and the artificial one, strengthening and making the realm of the self appear as the only one governing being.

In the mental sphere, it is feelings, the emotions and sensations, which play the role of the soul. Body and movements play the role of the lover. These facsimiles come to the forefront and become real for the mind sees them as such, but they cannot attain the level of fulfillment of the lover and the soul. Frustration is then double. First the self opposes by its very presence fulfillment, then creates a world where it can't be reached. This vicious circle, reflecting on the surface of a forgotten soul, with body, feelings and mind, this circle is more or less what we consider an individual.

21

A simple illustration would be that of a bubble. The air inside the bubble is the same as outside, but by enclosing it the bubble appears to be separating it from the rest, possessing it. The air would be experience, the bubble the mental dimension, and the air within the bubble our experience of the mental dimension, the world in which we spend most of our time.

So, having strayed, here we are in the bubble. Let's not forget that it is filled with air and very fragile. Once we are in it, it is easy to feel these walls harden, the air thicken, and to forget the sharp stab of death. Let's not forget that the reflecting self projects a seeming stability to a process constantly changing, that these walls are actually quite thin and transparent, and that when the bubble bursts, the artificial may find itself face to face with the consequences of its actions.

22

We are not trying here to condemn nor eliminate the mental dimension. We have in fact determined its basic altruistic nature and its honorable purpose, to eliminate pain. It is more like a process, a river meandering to the sea, creating all kinds of entities that took over and whose continued existence depends on not coming face to face with disturbing facts.

Yet understanding must evolve towards a wisdom which will reinstate harmony and make us no longer prey to pain. What is needed for this transformation to occur? The original problem lies in the neglect of the realm of lover and soul and in the way the self appropriated the energy of presence which animates being. The self must be emptied of this presence which must return to the entire creation and the world of understanding with all of its symbols must become just a reflection of the exchange between soul and lover. Understanding can go even a step further and grasp that lover and soul are but creations of the mind. It would thus transcend polarity, transcend mind in fact and bring being to a place where confusion no longer arises. That would be understanding's greatest achievement. The process that leads to these results is far from being dry and abstract. It is a saga, a true adventure within oneself, with an antagonist who though belonging to the world of symbols will reinstate harmony, out of love.

PART 2: THE FAMILY

In dried out parcels
the wheat is struggling to survive
while at a distance
the sun reflects
Upon the man made dam.

1

In this artificial world the part of us which acts, which moves, reflects the role of the lover who provided to the soul. In turn physical and emotional sensations play the part of the soul. Action now affects directly sensations and has become the provider. The bond between action and sensations mirrors the original bond of soul and lover. Here however the being of action must pass through the thought process before attempting to fulfill sensations, a thought process dictating action by imposing itself as knowing better, as true guide and protector.

This situation seems a bit abstract yet permits us to introduce entities which play a vital role in our present experience within this resultant dimension. Though until now we have named them "feelings", "thought", "action", "decision" and so forth, in truth they are entities similar to those in a family, and engage in ways which remind us of the conflict often found between generations, between youth and parents: Youth tends to focus on sensation and action, being less concerned with all the cares imposed by the parents for "planning and security". Living each day is more important, more natural. The woes of life also seem more immediate, not food for thought. In youth, action is the masculine element symbolized by a young boy with spontaneity and dynamism while sensations the feminine akin to a young girl, with delicacy in feelings and care in taste. We shall name here the young boy "the son", and the girl "the daughter."

2

On the other hand the mental aspect would be the parents: Her eye on the past, the mother interprets reality from the point of view of security. She watches over. She sees life's necessities and constantly concerns herself with the possible dangers to the children, in particular the daughter, and how to shield her. The father, in charge of the future, decides how to go about satisfying these needs in order to protect and sustain the family and steers the son in implementing those decisions.

What is presented here is a quick overview of the inner entities of the artificial world. In this way, we can look at it not in abstract terms but in terms of the relationships among members of a family. The importance of the family in human civilization could well be connected with its role in our basic inner constitution.

3

We can find many advantages to considering the inner constituents of being as members of a family. As long as we conceive of those elements as "the body", "the thought process", "emotions", "intent", the circle of self which consists of the "I"-"me" reflection containing a presence is practically impenetrable. In fact we usually see it as simply "me", the whole thing forged into one, and we even endow it with self-awareness, the illusion of a self knowing itself intrinsically without having to resort to the mirror where "me" is constantly reflected back. However, if we choose to fragment this "me" and set it on a family entity within us, we weaken it and start the process of dislodging presence so that it may return to the soul. Here identity will be with the son, in opposition to the "me" which tends to consider the father as the dominant entity as it is he who makes choices.

In addition, the simple fact that those entities are defined as members of a family makes them ipso facto relational by nature, existing solely in relationships. A father is so in so far as he relates to other members of the family. In fact young children do not imagine a person being there separate from the role. This relational quality brings us closer to original being and weakens even more the self by constantly thwarting its static appearance.

Finally, the apparent stability of the self blocks the energy of innate pleasure, the constant and vibrant soul-lover exchange. We first bring back this exchange as one between members of this family to eventually return it to its source, fissuring the stability of the self, its seeming autonomous existence. The exchange will be between son and daughter.

But really we consider elements of being as members of a family because it is an accurate view of things and can naturally lead to quick and deep inner transformation.

4

So with 4 entities on the stage of this artificial world, we have six different relationships: The daughter-mother relationship, and then those of mother-father, father-son, son-daughter, and also daughter-father, mother-son. These relationships control our lives and shape our personality.

If we examine them through the lens of the original and then the artificial, we can understand in great part the conflicts within us. We should not forget that these are created entities, reflections of the original base of being. So for example the daughter, who reflects the soul and thus the basis of being, has a different role here. She is source of pain and pleasure but not the fundamental layer of experience. She thus finds herself in a more vulnerable and precarious position. The son, in turn, who reflects the lover and thus the provider has his role basically snatched from him by the mental which appears as providing through him. He also loses his pedestal and ends up acting more like a messenger.

While original being aimed at fulfillment, this artificial family aims rather at happiness, its concept of it, pleasant physical and emotional sensations along with the mental sphere's satisfaction for any obtained solidity. Acquired though untold efforts any happiness nonetheless wavers and can at any moment slip away.

5

Artificial being tries to satisfy sensations and emotions through action, the son. As long as life is spontaneous the son does not consider is role a chore. He acts in a natural unopposed manner and the daughter responds, in a way very similar to children playing. But when with time spontaneous pleasure gives way to calculated pleasure, the son no longer acts on his own, the actions are no longer his. The mental, the parents, take over and he becomes subservient, losing touch with his natural energy. The relationship between son and daughter weakens away, with thought constantly lurking in between. Their bond remains deep but the continuity of the mental sphere, the existence of the parents itself depends on this space created between them. This transformation takes place progressively, relentlessly. Yet it is when this separation crystallizes that the romantic awakens and bursts, that the son and daughter rebel against mental flooding in a final effort to regain their lost kingdom of the spontaneous. They do so just like teenagers rebelling, to the great disarray of parents unable to understand and accept how uncontrollable their son or daughter has become. Similarly it is often at that time that one seeks a return to authenticity.

6

The son-daughter relationship is the only one reflecting the original lover-soul bond. The mother and father entities do not truly have counterparts in our original being. They arose from the effort of comprehension, thus in some way from the feedback process inherent in being as described earlier. In fact the father arose from the lover's doubt, and the mother from the soul's ensuing fear.

So from this son-daughter contact let's tackle the daughter-mother relationship, where the mother's role is to protect the daughter. She interprets reality in terms of what could possibly harm her daughter. This constant analysis diminishes the intensity of experience and ends up destroying all that is spontaneous. The daughter develops an ambiguous relationship with her mother: On one hand she appreciates the care, yet senses that her mother undermines the joy of life. The mother, who is constantly categorizing and attempting to keep the unpredictable at bay, wants her daughter to understand her and adopt her point of view. The bond between mother and daughter varies with each individual and culture and those who tend towards the mother's point of view often find themselves in an existence devoid of intensity, for the mother has eliminated all spontaneity and newness in life. The daughter may end up holding the mother responsible for this feeling of emptiness in her life.

Some of us refuse to bend to fear coupled with this kind of protection, and live a life where security is not queen. But for the most part individuals and societies adopt the mother's perspective. We need not look far for evidence: Young girls who, a few years back, lived fully in joys or sorrows of the moment and who's sole concern, fueled by fear of the unknown, is now their future and that of their family.

7

The other direct link the mother has is with the father. One's experience here is indeed shaped in two ways: First, as we just saw, through fear. Without fear, the daughter would have no reason to seek shelter in the folds of the mother. The other influence upon experience is action, thus the son. The mother, however, has no direct influence on the son. It's the father who does. Yet she does have a hold on the father, and can even shape the hold the father has on the son to make the son protect experience. Thus the bond between mother and father is to influence action. The mother amplifies fear and protection as the crucial element of existence. This element, spreading its influence, rules behavior in all spheres: It makes the father lead one towards greatest security, through his role of directing action. This principle of direction, of concentrated decision to shape the future by choosing a path of action for one's well being, this principle summarizes the father. By concentrating energies in a particular direction, he occupies a seat of strength and power and ends up controlling the action of the son. In fact the self tends towards him.

8

At times this feeling of power dominates the whole being. Nonetheless, it is its least alive part, giving birth to nothing, feeling nothing, conducting a task which can be frustrating and where failure often leads to anger.

The characteristics of the father, choice, decision, responsibility, control are closely linked to protective discrimination, the mother, upon whom they depend. Yet the father is only potential, for action does not necessarily follow choice. The influence the father has on the son is of crucial importance. The son can be compared to a wild horse free to roam at will finding himself tamed by a rider who dictates actions in all fields. This relationship between father and son is just as intimate as that of mother and daughter, though quite different.

With a clear perspective of the workings of these four aspects of being we understand how we function. Let us notice that there are two more links, mother-son and daughter-father which are indirect and thus whose effects are not as pronounced and more ambiguous.

9

This wheel that went into motion with the son-daughter link closes full circle with this direct father-son link.

The son can express a range of attitudes towards the father and the hold the father has on him. The amount of freedom he will seek will depend on how much he wishes to trust his own instinctive nature, where the purpose of the action is contained in the action itself and not in the mind attempting to bend it. Alas, acting in this way would put him in direct opposition with the mental dimension, the parents and even possibly with the daughter if she has been deeply influenced by the mother. Moreover in our technological world the son would have quite an arduous task leading the daughter to a desirable haven, bringing about pleasant sensations, without the help of the father. And yet his spontaneous energy is the only active link to the true dimension of being, the sole hope for a return to simplicity.

This wheel whirls unceasingly and shapes our present reality. A circle repeating itself with no respite, forgetting its origin and its relative, partial condition in the whole of being. At each instant these four factors join to shape our apparent experience. They picture themselves in an empty, hostile world. In fact, their very existence as well as that of their hostile world rose from the neglect and ensuing oblivion of the soul and from the transformation and ensuing paralysis the lover went through.

10

These four entities do not thrive on the role they play, far from it. It is a heavy, difficult one with few rewards. Most of the time sensations in a hostile environment are neither pleasant nor desirable. Protective discrimination is lined with fear. Choice becomes some sort of dictator while the role of the son is reduced to that of a worker, albeit a slave. Truth is hidden from them as well as any other alternative way of operating. Yet at times flutter the wings of a forgotten reality, the urge to access it. But how?

Fortunately this circle has its Achilles' heel for at the very moment of contact between son and daughter the mental ceases; slightly if the mental is in control, longer when the senses and the physical are at the forefront, yet at that time for an instant the mind is laid to rest and being's original conditions resurface. Hence each moment of our existence contains the replica of the direct contact between soul and lover. Though the conditions may not be desirable a continuity exists granting us an innate understanding, an instinctive aspiration towards the original state. Son and daughter meet, recognize each other, join, and then separate. Each time in them something yearns, yearns without end to no longer part.

11

So the mental settles in and the world of son and daughter which animates our experience in youth loses of its intensity as the mother analyzes the past and concerns herself much more with future events shaped by the father than with the experience of the present moment.

As contact between mother and father, between protection and choice strengthens, contact between son and daughter, action and sensation lessens, becomes more and more furtive. Originally meant to rescue the soul, the mental dimension, having long along buried true experience, now reduces the world of sensations to naught.

We can see this reflected in the way we take innumerable precautions through increasingly complex schemes and end up with practically no spontaneous, vibrant instants in life. Just as in our world adults never question this attitude which to them is obviously needed to deal with the uncertainty of life, within us the mental does not put into question its role and control. It just keeps on churning away and our experience is more or less experience of the mental sphere to the expense of the son-daughter dimension. What we end up with is a son and daughter adapted to the dictates of the mental sphere, a body and sensations willfully bowing to the world of fear. Yet just as sensations go through experience, the mental must go through sensations, and each little instant a son-daughter meeting, no matter how slight, maintains the continuity of basic experience traced from its origin all the way here.

12

Let us take someone on the way to work, driving in an automatic fashion while the mind is going through events, giving them meaning and then getting lost in their possible consequences, in the way they may unfold, what to do so that they would enfold the right way, what to fear if they don't... this is the relationship that rules, this exchange where past and future erase the present, where the mental sphere shadow sensation, where the mother and the father unite instead of son-daughter. This lack of living the moment is the faded contact between son and daughter, the subjugation of what pleasure their union can give, the condemnation of the simplicity of their world, the domination of the daughter by the mother, the domination of the son by the father, the fear of acting spontaneously, the fear of action devoid of thought, the dread of pure pleasure and of what it could lead to, foolish acts, losses, fear and pain, all that the parents are trying to avoid and which makes them replace "be" by "plan" and for what? Or really, for whom? For the daughter? She finds herself wilted, hoping even for some real pain devoid of concern to know herself again, to see herself, to know who she is, the daughter and not the mother, the present and not the past, nor the future, nor the virtual experience of the mental sphere, but the true experience of her lover, the body, that he may come again even for an instant live in her, vibrate in her, transpierce the mind, make it shut up, and for an instant feel, really feel her world rise again, this world slipping under her feet, this world of pleasure which surrounds and terraces, where mind departs, dies, and with it all limitations. We have it here, the birth of sex, and the death of childhood.

13

This rebellion lasts but an instant, dies out, and the mental sphere takes over again. However another current, slow and subtle, could be set in motion, that of the daughter and son wishing to regain control. This desire to join, to no longer be parted by mental events unites them in a desperate cause. The daughter emanates her refusal to no longer be dominated by the mother. But it is the son who must get back control of the energies. It is not a matter of eliminating the mental sphere, but of subduing it. He can do so because all that manifests is in its barest aspect motion, action, thus really is the son, mental manifestations included. For this reason he can weaken and even halt the flux of thoughts simply by controlling their manifestation, rather than getting duped by their content. When he does, roles get reversed: the mental, who was the rider, is now a creature out of control being tamed and showing its compulsive, self preserving aspect. Holding the reins, maintaining mental silence, the son curbs the father. At times the son can even make the mental stop its compulsive flow and start telling it where to go.

14

This is an inner meditation for silence and peace. The son is letting the father know that his demands can no longer suppress experience of the moment. In the same way the daughter lets her mother know she no longer wishes fear to reduce the range and intensity of sensations. Experience centers more and more on the present, on its continuity. The mental sphere, of course, resists whenever it can, distracting, arguing, trying to dissuade, thus demanding from the part of son-daughter a continued effort to maintain their hold. Moreover the environment works with the mental as today's world mirrors its vision of things. This effort is not an easy task but those attempting it usually quickly recognize its worth and will do all they can not to lose contact with this burgeoning spontaneity, leading the way to a much deeper and important step to integrity.

Being able to remain more in the present brings about well being but the mental sphere is always ready to call an alarming situation where an apparent need for self-preservation will permit it to take over. Rare are those who can maintain it constantly at bay, usually at the price of an extremely simplified life. Others revert to a balancing act, holding the mental sphere at bay through meditative disciplines such as dance or art where concentration on the moment is crucial or where the body's movement supersedes that of the mind. Yet the mental sphere's assertion that it offers protective self-interest permits it to regain again and again its hold on being.

15

In this world where the mental dominates, the well being of a harmonious son-daughter link recalls our original state but it is limited by the conditions which brought it about: the loss of the original sphere, the alienation of the soul and finally the creation of a reality of concepts in which we operate. Those able to hold in check the mental and who know the joy this brings about glimpse at the possibility of extracting the harmful element from the mental sphere, of neutralizing it and even transforming it so that thoughts would be more like companions on a journey. Even the vulnerability that serves as a motor to the mental sphere could be overcome. For some a forgotten shore whispering from the depth of their being leads them on. Calm and silence allowed them to feel what the mental sphere was constantly attempting to cover up through ceaseless activities, this sadness, this loss emanating from faraway lands within, a disturbing echo to their newly found enjoyment. What is it? Who is it? What does it have to tell us?

16

The strong son-daughter bond reconnected to the forgotten experiencer, the soul. Though alienated from the incomprehensible and frightful new reality the mental sphere created, the soul cannot completely detach herself from it for it is tied to it by existence itself. She hid, and the darkness and isolation she found herself in solidified the new artificial reality we described. She has but aversion towards the self, the entity in the artificial world which took the place of her lover. However, as she shapes creation, no matter how flattering this self is to itself, underneath it is tainted with the soul's view of it and covered with shame.

Would it be possible to get rid of it? This daring proposition is not as impossible as it seems. When the self is useful, it seems indispensable. When its usefulness is gone, it turns into a ghost lurking in the structure of being. Yet only by reuniting soul and lover can we truly eliminate it. At that moment the energy of the self will stop haunting and return to its source. For this reconciliation to occur reason is not enough, it is not understanding alone which will convince the soul to once again trust the one who seemingly betrayed her. One must make use of a certain emotional intelligence, learnt through human relations, which tells us what to do to merit again her trust. It's this trust that will make her leave her hiding place and know once again her lover, ending his exile.

This movement toward the center of being, repenting, reparation, acceptance, is what we usually term as "religion".

PART 3: THE PATH

My loved one is alone far away
Known only to her tear.
Though you see me
How can I be here?

This path is presented as experienced by a man
A woman is bound to travel it differently

1

Thinking of the soul in human terms with our logic will not do, she knows nothing of it, no way to convince her with words. Here we are dealing with the kind of truth children know, when adults' words contradict their way of being and children see it so clearly. Words appear to the soul as objects tinted by their content, not by what they mean to represent. Music lies less but silence is definitely the language of truth. Silence permits man to recognize the dead-end he got carried into. Silence is dropping the blade which carves savagely a future. Silence is wishing to no longer hear oneself constructing reasons. Silence is the wish to reach this empty space which will suck out of us all these crowding thoughts, condemning yet finding no blame with themselves, which in silence become so heavy, heavy as words, followed by thoughts repressed until now and which need to air in the silence and if we let them they could find their own silence and cease, all these pent up thoughts, to give way to images, all these images piled behind thoughts, sharp, these images that enlighten without words, show us without saying a thing, and which finally give way to a void and a hollowness which conspire to crack a rock, the rock of all our ideas, a crack through which seeps a spring, a stream, a voice, words that transpierce the silence yet no one is speaking, a quiet voice we hearken to with fingers clutching hope.

2

But really, we must backtrack to know who is listening to this voice, who laid to the ground the weapons of mind to follow depth in feelings, who turned towards this distress so close yet far, intimate yet nowhere. Who in us roams the silence, searches its confines, forgets the words and tunes in to the faraway melody?

Let's return to when the son, opposing the father's will, curbs the mental and its hold on him. At that moment a being resurfaces, the antithesis of this world, a son for whom action lies in inaction, movement in stillness, wisdom in silence, and where the far limits of our world are found within. A son facing the desolation of a love plundered with beings dancing to the rhyme of the scythe over its tomb. A son who will stretch his arms out in a desperate effort to reach to both parts of being and bridge them. Then he will let himself dissolve into the silence from which he came so that they may embrace. He does this for one reason: he is loving care, he is the altruist reborn.

3

Returning to the source, we recall the altruist as he who, realizing the soul's pain and wishing to soothe her, divided himself to understand. He surfaces when the original conditions reappear and maintains his essential nature: wishing to fulfill the soul. He awakens to the consequences of his act, torn by what he sees without knowing quite how it happened. He cannot but throw himself in the task of restoring what was, led by a wisdom and a guide, by a mother and father from the feedback system who, thank God, did not lose it, tracing a path with intuitive words, thoughts and visions. A path which takes him to the depths of being, altering his whole way of thinking, of seeing and acting to loosen the hold the world of symbols has on him. A path beyond this newly acquired spontaneity of action, leading to the freedom of the soul strayed for having followed him in illusion and reaping its bitter fruits. To the freedom of she who in natural passivity is the bed of this vessel called life as he knows himself to be its sides, the bottom of this life in which experiences pile up, in which we bury all that displeases us to maintain the pleasant on the surface, without ever wanting to see that which in the depth of us suffers from lack of love, care and comprehension, and by pushing her back we push time ahead, we feed and nourish it, we make it come alive by rejecting she who is alone, soiled and abandoned, miserable and cursed, the rejection of the one he loves, this son just reborn, his reason for being, his soul, Sorrow.

4

Sorrow, who are you? No doubt you guide our actions, for what we do, we do to escape you. We do our best to seal and conceal you and yet here you are, as rooted as ever in our lives. You seem as distant as our first memories and certain to accompany our last. In a changing world you remain a constant, in this solid world you elude us. Though source of all our actions, you don't act, you feel, you lay still and react. Sorrow, I believe you are she who must endure the self, bound to this self who attempts by all means to escape from you, casting you away as wrecked.

Yet fear not for his reign is coming to an end for here is the one who will take his place, take your hand, the one to whom you belong truly, who will stand facing you, the portal to your deliverance. You must recognize him, care for him lest he wanders without end. Pull away from the self with his loveless presence, from his strength carved in violence, don't mistake what he is and thus fail to recognize your helper, fail to give him life, fail to sustain and guide him as one guides one blinded, blinded yet with such a finely tuned ear, finely tuned to your melodies, Sorrow, to the melody of all that remains true, the melody of what you really are, Sensitivity.

5

I say as a blind man for indeed to continue his trail he must split away from the reality of thoughts, no longer be prey to dictates of thought and ensuing action. He is different. A thought comes forth, he does not look at where it wants to lead him. Rather, he tries to grasp the effect it has on she who feels thoughts, where thoughts lose themselves to make room for others, the surface each thought stings as it turns to action. He does not act, he remains with each traveling thought, uses it as a mount, a mount bringing him to the one he wishes to know better, to step on her shore and listen to her ripples. However, to resist getting caught up in thoughts he pays no attention to the logic guiding them, to the reasoning connecting them, to the practicalities they point to. He is in fact blind to the course of the world, which permits him to get closer to you, to be with you while others are so busy attempting to erase you.

6

You see them all scrambling ceaselessly on the surface of things, all under the spell of the self to forget you, to replace you with feelings of pleasure, each one another sprout attempting to reach happiness by being furthest from you. And then you see him alone, clearing a way to you, coming closer, beginning to guess what kind of world you live in, wishing to know you, it scares you. It scares you because sorrow does not wish to know itself, you also wish to escape, live illusions as much as possible, live in others running away from you, but here he is at your shore, drawing you to yourself, bringing up all the harm done, what for? What good will his presence do, though he is the first to come close, of what use is it? In what way can it help? Let me sink in forgetfulness, let me be hypnotized by those who have forgotten me, hypnotized by their laughter; this you say, but in your own language, which has neither thought nor awareness, just waves.

Would there be another reason for fearing his presence? After all here he is coming to you full of good intentions and you shudder, as from fear of punishment. Why? Would it be that one of your sorrows is guilt, guilt that because of suffering men hurt others, thus multiplying the miseries of mankind? You would then be the beginning and the end of this vicious cycle they cannot escape, and you dread retribution. So you hide even more, hide that you feel, hide that you live, you become even more of a shadow, the fleeting shadow that punctuates our every step.

7

Until when will you endure this torture? Isn't it time to stop, to open up to help? The one you see turning your way cannot harm you, will not betray you nor judge you, he will be able to remain steadfast with you no matter what. He will have kindness. He will listen to your tears and will hear the gentle flow, and in this gentle flow you will recognize yourself and know that you have done nothing, that suffering is the cloth this world is making you wear to bind you. He will help cease the flight of time to bring back dazzling timelessness. Yet now he needs you, needs you to lower your veil, needs you enter this gateway he unlocks to the end of pain.

8

Already he is out of the clutches of thoughts and guided by an intuitive force where care is king and original reality seeps in. Yet the strength of the self weigh heavy upon him and with the "me" he must play a double game. He must understand it to fight it yet to not sway to habits he must act in an altruistic fashion, or not at all.

To act altruistically he would help others but this could keep him in the world of ideas. One form of altruistic action however never discourages and leads straight to his goal, and yours: To see in all guess who: you and only you. When he gives, he gives to you. He lives following your shadow, our world's shadow and never stops wishing for others to recognize it too.

The others, where do they come from? You saw them emanate just like thoughts from ignorance of original reality, all imbued with fear and with you at the heart, all with the purpose of avoiding pain yet to bring pain to an end rather than free you they bury you, alive. In their ways they are so diverse, entertaining even, yet in their purpose they are all the same, just a reflection of one another and what they do not understand is that though they are so diverse their pain is not, their suffering is the same, you, Sorrow, the same in all.

9

At first you pay very little attention to him, you are rather frightened. Yet slowly, you can't stop making him the center of your attention. His simplicity, goodwill and perseverance form such a contrast with the hubbub tainted with bitterness that surrounds others. When you center on him, you cannot deny an instant of respite quite different from forgetting. An instant of peace flowing, a room, a shelter from the world, a place in short where you feel acceptance. Why, though, would he accept suffering, why seat you here, you and your heavy burden, so far away from lightness, why treat you with such respect and even affection while others trample you, why seek you while others flee, what is driving him, making him brave the current, making him tie this weight to his ankle which pulls him so far from time flowing to the throes of self and of times gone by? Could he actually be seeking the heart of sorrow, could he possibly dive so deep without drowning, could he bear the pain, the pressure on all parts, and even if he does reach this black hole, your heart, even if you yield, what would he do there, how could he be of help and what seed would he place that could change anything? But really, you have nothing to lose your waves whisper while you get more and more used to offering him your presence, letting him explore, all the while with a gnawing question: Why?

10

The seed he will lay, you sowed it yourself without knowing it. How could your tears sow anything? They can, for being the soul in the universe of the bubble, whether the others know it or not, you hold the creative power, the only one in our world who cannot get lost in the illusion that this world could replace the true one, you who cannot make believe, you who knows not how to lie, and so you in whom our mystery resides. This creative power heard your tears and prayers. From it sprouted the path of return in forms diverse. A path that is none but your true parents coming to your rescue, through their son. He comes to you as branches reach for light, it's his nature, he knows what he is doing, he is making love, and bringing you death.

Yes, death, you know it well for it goes hand and hand with the suffering of our world. You feel them all ask, demand, beg for just a bit more sieve, these old leaves, but the sieve goes to the younger, they fall and nothing remains of them but the crackling of your steps on autumn paths that those swaying in the wind hearken to with fright. Yes death, you know it well, but yours, Sorrow, your death, to no longer be sorrow, could you accept it? Will you take the gift he has for you, his gift of deliverance? Let us know, Sorrow, when you are ready to go, having suffered so.

11

Here he is then, the fruit of your prayers. All is set, his time is spent listening to the voice of wisdom, changing, getting ready for the task at hand. He knows himself to be part of the artificial world, filled by the confusions of this world, imbued by this "me" no matter what, in the flow of time, of change. You, he senses, have a hold on the other part, in your eternity, on the half that permits being. Together, becoming and being will no longer contradict each other, they will complement each other. Until now becoming reaped suffering, the shadow of any form it takes, the projection of its confusion. And now he is ready and willing to join this shadow and mingle with it.

12

Yet the task is enormous: How can a changing world join a timeless one? They cannot wed, they seem condemned, he to wander trying to seize a reflection, she bewildered by these movements with no heads or tail which nonetheless hypnotize her. He the ship without anchor, she the ocean with no destination. For she touches all shores while here he is, crisscrossing from one place to another in a straight or curved line, yet what determination, what energy in this blind dance, this illusion of time is enticing but beyond her reach unless...is it possible, has he found the means to join them? He does something so simple and natural: He takes time and transforms it. He takes time and puts it in a book. This book opens and closes, time opens and closes, it belongs to both for she holds the book from cover to cover while he lives it, but he does not live it like others, he lives it not as a real thing but as a thing magical, as a story, this story he fashioned that she first reads, then lives, and when she will read the last pages, when she will live them they will fold back into a medallion that she will carry unto her breast, a medallion which is nothing more than his eyes, his way of seeing the world, his care.

13

What did he need to do to transform his world into a story? First he had to know someone would read it, that someone was reading it, that you were here, witness to all that occurred, distanced, silent but present. That you had to be brought back into this world that pushed you away, your rightful place had to be found and offered to you. He knew you were here, present and not something to avoid. Then he simplified his life, letting go of everything that could throw you off, all these false words, all these mental fabrications you could not relate to. He paid attention only to that which was accompanied by a note, note of a melody that went hand in hand with the story, that you could listen to and welcome.

14

If he seems to be running after something, he does it because he knows that is his role, he does it intuitively but in truth he is only running after you, he does not hesitate to suffer, incorporates pain and thus you. He eliminates the rejection that colored the soul. For these reasons you let yourself go, you hesitate less, you hide less. He feels your presence, it grows, guides him, directs him. Feeling suffering recognized, feeling suffering accepted, feeling sorrow given solace you liberate yourself from it and while it flows you lighten. It's hard but you change, less hurt, less of a victim more of a spectator. You get closer to your source while suffering settles in this story, becomes part of the story, without you, it is emptied of you for you are now the reader. You hold in your hands the book of life, of the life of he who is playing well his role. Meanwhile suffering, not finding you, tears him apart. Yet he offers it no home and it ends up becoming stings and pains with no core, no continuity, no soul, part of the story, the rags which covered you which now cloth nobly his offered body, a body transmuted by unimaginable gratitude. It transmutes the blood flowing in and from his veins into nectar, this gratitude, it answers all his questions, your immense and eternal gratitude, it is the beginning of your love.

15

One day finally you open to him. One day when thoughts and even hints of thoughts lay frozen in some winter landscape, he tumbles and finds himself on the other side. He becomes you, without words, in some eternity, in experience only, his body that of a woman, the feeling of being a woman and sees himself as you have always seen him, for an instant in your world he sees himself as you know him and have always known him with no inside, the inside was only the mind's madness with no meaning to you but which kept you hypnotized to his reality, this reality that sees its last day, its last instant, for you both wake up, you from your hypnosis, he from his madness, just the time of a kiss. Then he seems to be only you, he is gone, he became you, he is but a memory, your reality now takes over, you are, and for the first time you know you are, woman somehow, out of the world awakened from a long sleep, from a nightmare seemingly with no beginning, it's thanks to him, you don't know how but it's thanks to him and though he is now gone you love him.

16

But he is not gone. Just as you had been the backdrop of his life, the canvas upon which it took form, so did he become your background, but this canvas was his vision of you, his love for you, a world where you could be again without getting lost, where you could find yourself. On this canvas, miracle you can move, on this canvas, miracle nothing hurts, on this canvas, miracle you feel so deeply something you knew so well, Love.
Then the world calls him back, his man's body calls him despite himself, he retakes shape and slowly returns, returns to his world, returns to this world which does not know it yet but has just lost its basis of existence.

He knows now, in his gut he knows that this world has no true foundation, functions mistakenly, rests and depends on your bewilderment.

17

He retraces his steps. He recounts how he devoted himself to reach the origin of sorrow, how he immersed himself in this quest toward you the moment he realized that you were his own companion in prey to the miseries of the "me" because of him. Seeing none but you, being only with you, he built a bridge between you so that you may touch and join. He built it by giving meaning only to what concerned you both, seeing in everything simply what concerned you both. He spanned it by seeing you in all, by acting as if you were following each of his moves, weighing them, and flowing more and more with them.

18

At first it was a difficult role to play for he could neither feel nor seize your presence, just guess it through some intuition he had. Difficult to play also for it demanded the negation of his existence's usual footholds. He recalls seeing drifting out of sight the reference points he lived by, so as to make room for your story. As long as you were Sorrow, the role was taxing and solitary, requiring constant effort. But once you were drawn in, you started living the story freely. He sensed this change through ease in his movements, in his way of being, less resistance, less effort. Then his gestures lightened up, thoughts floated, choice seemed less constraining, feelings flowed, the role was much easier to play and then one day you welcomed him, he became you, the altruist died in you and only the lover remained. When he returned he was no longer the same, he no longer believed anything, he no longer believes in anything.

19

He retakes his place, feeling empty, existing neither here nor there. The story seems over. He knows he cannot return to before. In truth, it does not interest him. The world of their story is much more real than the world he left behind, this existence much more authentic to his nature. Moreover now a gentle energy does not cease penetrating him, a subtle inner trembling that takes hold of each atom and animates it into a soft simmering of well being. He wakes up each morning accompanied by this flow of delight which he sees as their union. Letting go of an old skin he now identifies with this exquisite energy and in this way gives back both body and mind to creation.

He feels, he knows from his experience that not only him but all that surrounds him is known to her, exists certainly not as the former harsh and lifeless world but in her eyes, however she does not have any so in her heart, yet the heartbeats that resounded so clearly fade, fade into the fluttering of wings, light, quivering, then one day nothing, past all turmoil, she broke through to the other side, to her home, reduced to infinity, no trace of her.

20

Peace, one could say, yet in this silence, this vast silence, he knows she surrounds him, she accompanies him. He accepts it, he resigns himself to this new kind of love. He does what is left for him to do: others, she in others, here is the task at hand. Yet now, he can only recall what sorrow is, who Sorrow was. It's as if she never existed, as if all had just been a fantasy. He explores the edge of the story, nothing, no jetty, no framework to venture out, comes back and settles without the least idea of what is waiting for him, unaware of the transformation ahead. He does not know she has taken over to finish stripping him of the remnants of the self so that he too may return to where he belongs. Having devised for her an escape from this world of manifestations, she will now care for him from the unseen realm, she will etch the paths for them. He is unaware that her silence reflects a reality far different from his, a universe which will embrace him, a naturally encompassing love to which he will surrender and which will magically bring him back to his true home, theirs.

PART 4: TRANSFORMATION

She is a flow unbroken
My eyes cannot blink
My mind cannot scheme
So smooth, so silky, so soft
and shimmering
around the silvery moon's journey
through hollowness.

1

It would be difficult to gage when control started slipping away, perhaps when choice appeared more and more ludicrous. He acted yet felt he was doing nothing. He thought, yes, and accordingly would act, yes, yet right there and then another consciousness would come to the forefront to ridicule this preamble to spontaneity. Thoughts and acts alike would parade along well defined routes and even an unpredictable turn felt familiar in a present that would not give way to future, a very old, limitless present, her preventing him from leaving her towards the world of the made-up, of the planned, of the mental. The soul returns to the sphere of the bubble, this time not bewildered, and adds spontaneity to all actions, basic spontaneity overwhelming through its unbelievable lightness the weight of all decisions, for in fact the goal has already been attained. The actor who still weighs the stakes at hand is like a player still playing after the game is over, the goal scored, the bell rung, all his efforts matter not while the silence of the crowd accentuates the ridicule of those efforts which until now had appeared so serious and determined. Slowly the "me" is stripped of the element of choice which gave it so much power and to which the rest of being yielded. It becomes a passive self, perceiving but not acting. As for the lover, he now grasps that the layers that constitute the self are about to be peeled one by one and lends himself to this subtle play. He senses that the way to emancipate Sorrow in others is to integrate himself fully to this dimension where he ceases acting, and sees himself effortlessly going along with it. In love he becomes a prisoner of life.

2

To live without choice is not as radical as it may seem. It is not a matter of not having a role to play. Choice is a conception, the idea that at each moment an element comes into play transcending the conditions and their consequence, not part of the conditions, an element to which us human beings attribute our semi-divinity, which makes us masters, in the castle of "me the master". But his home is now his story, and he can pull back and see how choice evolves, how it serves as a main trigger for the mechanism of the self to be set in motion, how it separates.

Thus he still acts but lacking the element of choice, he follows a road that does not lead to a labyrinth but to integration of action and inaction, to a dimension where one does without acting, where one acts when doing nothing. In this newly found freedom of doing without acting he contemplates the landscape, the subtle elements of the inner landscape. He sketches in the horizon the silhouette of she who was sorrow and now rises as peace within peace extirpating him from the chaos he gave rise to in trying to help her.

3

Past this first confusion an element which in fact triggered choice and seems even more unquestionable sharpens, vulnerability. Yet what gave vulnerability life was the crack between the two intimate parts of being and what it produced: the mental sphere with its capacity to harm them. Now communication is flowing and direct, does not go through the mental, nourishes no one else. Stripped of its driving force, vulnerability can no longer function. It remains still, the weight of an existence, so heavy that the bottom of the container defining it gives way, vulnerability drops and drowns in the immensity of well-being. So now whenever he sets foot in a place of seeming fragility, it is well being that submerges him instead, while vulnerability dissipates, joining its source, sensitivity.

4

Just like with choice, this may seem a bit incongruous. We all know ourselves to be vulnerable, our body is vulnerable and so is our fate, pain is all around, the future can unleash such misery. To call oneself invulnerable in such conditions simply seems to show that one has lost touch with everyday life and its obvious precarious predicament. But we must understand what kind of vulnerability we are speaking of here. Let's compare life to a vessel on an ocean. If it has a hulk that cannot crack, it will not sink. It will face storms, yes, yet it is invulnerable in the sense that it will not sink. So with the human heart, the joining of the two parts of our being, their direct communication, their partial return to their basic state produces a constant energy of well-being coupled with an instinctive knowledge that whatever experiences lie ahead, whatever the whims of the sea of life, the shell floating to the sway of experience will no longer sink, water will not seep in. In fact we have here a great theme of romantic literature and poetry: If only the two lovers could overcome adversity, could truly unite, all hostile forces would lose their hold on them, their reality would last "forever" against obstacles. We know this "forever" is just a word, the body dies, yet if it is used, it's because it reveals our heart's deep intuition, that if the two parts that form one heart would unite and fuse, allegorically if the blood flowed directly from one to the other, it would be forever, the heart could navigate the worst of conditions on its way but really already home.

5

Having left far behind the world he belonged to, he must acknowledge as he watches life's foundations disintegrating and crashing piece by piece into the ocean that what he thought was the end of a story was a beginning, that all he had done and from which he drew some pride was a prelude. The feminine now holds the helm leading being to fulfillment, not in an active way which is the way he knew but rather through osmosis, through her surrounding presence comforting and absorbent, through an osmosis that worries not of time nor of storms nor of the refusals of the mind, it can't be, no it can't, I cannot toss overboard what I hold as the heart of being, the core of me, and yet he knows it is just a matter of time, of slowly eroding resistance, it's just a matter of time, she already has me, knows me, does not judge me, she knows him, she does not judge him. Just as he had at one point played the role of the father, here she is playing that of the mother, she knows better, she loves unconditionally, she waits, she surrounds with attention, never judges, she watches with limitless affection the transformation of a confused self.

6

Having lost sight of the coastline, he drifts yet knows he is in good hands. He also knows he is entering hollowness, that all that still sustains him is about to give way, the role he played is about to melt, pangs of the heart will mark time, he cannot conceive the end of this transformation, he cannot conceive not conceiving. How did she manage to get used to it with such ease, with none of those fears assailing her? For her, its true, being hollow is natural. Moreover she had him, she had his presence to hold on to if need be, while he never saw her face. It was relatively easy for her to settle in nonbeing, she had him, being, but he, he has only hollowness to hold on to, and being is dissipating.

7

With vulnerability and choice vanishing in the distance another part of his constitution crystallizes, a part which seems to have given him birth, guided him, defined him: Purpose. Indeed, all that he has done until now in such a natural and intuitive fashion he did it because his goal spurted out effortlessly, his raison d'être forged in him, impossible to remove it without removing his very skin and yet suddenly she whom he was helping and to whom he had devoted himself seems to need him no longer, in fact the opposite is occurring, really he no longer has a reason for being except perhaps just to be. He is naturally pulled to helping others, to help her in others, that was the goal he had set for himself henceforth. Yet reality took an ironic turn. There was a time when sorrow and all that came with it formed a solid dimension, a dimension all attempted to avoid but still a guide for action. Now this suffering in others seems fleeting for that's how he feels, it is fleeting to him. The longer time carries him away from what he used to know, the harder it is for him to conceive of the solidity of the pain others go through, he senses a sort of space-time distortion there rather than a gravitational center. In fact he can no longer imagine in them the self he used to know in him. It was after all but a belief and so even more so the self he assumed in others. Truly his deep sadness arises from what is so clearly missing in this world and permeates his, innate bliss born of innate love capable of counteracting great distress. A bliss which does nothing but glitter, and at times shine.

8

So on one hand he goes along with helping those who do not see otherwise but on the other hand he glimpses at the dimension that would blossom without him, without his intervention, this dimension he cannot define as other than sublime-ness. In the world with others there may be a place for him, but in his none, and to find a refuge in the role that others give him would be a subterfuge. He acknowledges the end of purpose, its vanishing, while being transformed by the presence of she who is now not only peace but wisdom, a wisdom that strips him so skillfully of the scaffold the mental sphere erected. He gradually witnesses his actions arise magically by themselves, his floating thoughts lose both origin and direction. He sees an existence devoid of essence within a sphere of pure pleasure.

9

Here he is then without raison d'être and for the first time clearly surfaces the source of his being, the reflection he sprouted from. For the first time his perception devoid of direction and movement remains rooted to him and he cannot avoid the obvious: perceiving himself creates his presence, the mind's principal task is to perceive himself. Everything flows from this reflection, this deeply rooted habit, buried deep and practically impossible to unearth: to live with oneself, to become so familiar with oneself, to be one's constant companion, a place to cozily nestle knowing our companion will not rattle anything as we get along so well in this lair where we never cease concerting each other, the most powerful to the most miserable of beings do exactly the same thing, in a palace or on hay, they find there the same comfort.

10

Most do not realize they do so, but he does, he also knows this occurred the moment the lover questioned himself, dividing himself thus giving rise to an awareness seemingly capable of abstracting itself from experience to view or direct it. Doing so created a construct, an awareness that could exist outside of experience, our present awareness.

What to do now, eliminate it? This would be neither possible nor desirable. What is needed is to expose and confound the fallacy that this awareness can operate out of experience, in fact that it exists out of experience, that it is not part of experience. The one way to do so is to permit the soul, his soul mate in the proper sense of the word who is about to become pure experience, to take back everything, to conquer back her kingdom. She, from her side, simply asks him to pull away from the mirror, to throw overboard this part of himself always in the habit of thinking that it is he rather than she who knows him, to give up the idea that each parcel of his body and spirit resonates in him rather than in her, finds basis in the mirror of the mind rather than in the depth of experience.

She asks but in fact no, she does not ask anything as really he can no longer do anything. Yes, she does ask him not to resist, to resist as little as possible, to go with the stream, to not hinder the splendor of the transformation, to maintain an obliging smile as he fragments.

Pierced from all sides until the last bastions of his identity float on an ocean that has encompassed him, he lets pleasure supplant him.

11

Encompassed by experience, what does that really mean? It simply means that one no longer dwells in abstractions, that the mind no longer has that blackboard, that black slate on which it erected its realities and its plans. All that is flows directly from experience and goes right back to it, feelings of course but also thoughts, questions, answers, concerns, impressions, friends, loved ones even, the body, the experience of a body, the body's experience, all emanate, spring out of experience, flood the moment in successive waves that leave no room, no time for constructs. Life is lived that way, it's a different system but it works, it is synchronized to wisdom and finally, crucially, the taste of ecstasy is never far. Awareness could no longer maintain its ramparts, it let go, shattered and scattered, no more center, then returned subdued, knowing it did not have the answer. Now it simply echoes experience, becomes its lining, clothes Experience with names, with words.

12

There was something else, an abstraction even greater than this black slate: the core, the nucleus of the self, at the heart, black also, all of life gravitated around it, choice, vulnerability, intention and existence, a kind of unfathomable black hole which provided the certainty that one existed, a kind of control hub with a fixed presence. He knew it very well, that pit, and each time he felt he reached a new place, a new horizon, he hoped it would no longer be there, but no, here it was again and again, so tenacious, emanating steadily this feeling of presence, forcing him to return to himself, to this self still and out of time that makes one believe that it will be there always, that makes believe in the soul and its eternity, that even passes for it. Ironically it is the soul that gave it birth, in the way things give birth to colors, absorbing all but the visible one, rejecting the color we actually perceive. In the same way, the rejected part of the lover's brightness was reflected back and the constancy of the rejection formed an impression of steadiness which solidified, gained enormous mass around which we now gravitate. For him though, the mirror was no longer, the shut door of rejection had instead opened wide, this portal, this soul. What remained was but a vestige.

13

And then one day, in the lobby of a hotel with fifteen minutes to kill, he looked at himself, he looked for the pit and found inside only the reflection of the moment's experience. The center of gravity was gone, the planets were free. Outside was reflected inside, what was occurring at the moment was mirrored where the core used to be, nothing more.

And now feelings, but also thoughts, questions, answers, concerns, impressions, friends, loved ones even, the body, the body's experience, the experience of a body, all find no center to solidify around and simply run through him more like waves, to the taste of pleasure fulfilled. Experience encompassed him, leaving him de-localized, un-localizable.

PART 5 : THE HAVEN

A shadow in the land of scarcity
A thrill in the land of plenty
Where the eye does not see
My half-self is but
A fleeting memory

True pleasure is an inner vibration. From love's tuning fork rang out a note which never ceased spreading. Now the whole being vibrates with pleasure, and does so no matter what. This pleasure is the regained domain of soul and lover and we can certainly grasp why it would consist of a vibration since a vibration is a continuous back and forth movement.

This domain of lover and soul, this sea of churning pleasure now goes hand in hand with the wisdom of a wise mind whose self-understanding ended any interference. With no reason for being, this mind throws itself into this sea, focusing solely on vibrant pleasure.

One day, on a hilltop, I suddenly started spinning and, letting go, I swirled faster and faster. My legs had acquired a dazzling rhythm and were moving on their own. Suddenly I had the sensation that I was no longer moving. The world, however, the world around me was now turning, spinning madly, while I felt I was simply standing, with no connection to my feet which were stamping the ground at a crazed tempo. An immense peace came over me, an endless relief.

In the same way, the mind inundated by this pleasure operates yet no longer moves. Its creations, the soul and lover, fade away, just experience remains. Meanwhile the energy of pleasure ceases being seen as an exchange between them. Rather, inside becomes outside then inside again, giving turns to receiving and again to giving. The energy of pleasure spins unobstructed, beyond grasping, encompassing all realities. It becomes woman, than man, then woman again, disappearing in pleasure, to reappear memory.

Made in the USA
Columbia, SC
08 January 2024